CRIBBAGE

IS THE NAME OF THE GAME

the text of this book is printed
on 100% recycled paper

CRIBBAGE
IS THE NAME OF THE GAME

Richard E. Lowder

BARNES & NOBLE BOOKS
A DIVISION OF HARPER & ROW, PUBLISHERS
New York, Hagerstown, San Francisco, London

The tuck case on the cover design is used with permission of The United States Playing Card Company.

First BARNES & NOBLE BOOKS edition published 1974.

LIBRARY OF CONGRESS CATALOG CARD NUMBER: 74-7671

STANDARD BOOK NUMBER: 06-463402-7

77 78 79 80   12 11 10 9 8 7 6 5 4 3

CONTENTS

INTRODUCTION

This is a book for people who play cribbage and also for people who would like to learn more about the game. If you are an experienced cribbage player, think of the many games that you have lost by a few pegs. The important thing to realize is that the difference between an expert player and an average player is very slight, and this difference can be accounted for by the fact that the expert player takes advantage of every possible opportunity.

Cribbage is one of the most widely played card games in the United States and Canada. Hundreds of thousands of people participate in friendly home games, and many take part in organized league play.

There are several reasons for the widespread interest in the game of cribbage.

▲ The use of the cribbage board and pegging involves the players directly and continually in the game. Each player is readily able to observe and monitor his game progress.

▲ Cribbage belongs to the meld family of card games, and therefore provides numerous chances to score points through many different combinations such as pairs, fifteens, and runs.

▲ On the surface, cribbage looks easy to learn and simple to play. However, as this book will reveal, this is not necessarily correct. The rules are easy to learn, but additional knowledge

1

and experience are required in order to play the game in a scientific manner.

▲ Cribbage has great spectator appeal. Because the cribbage board and score are readily visible, passersby can quickly evaluate game progress and determine who is leading. And players unconsciously like to be the center of attention.

Although cribbage is very popular, little has been published about it in comparison with the many books that are available on other card games, such as poker and bridge.

This book outlines the rules of play, but more important, it provides helpful guidelines on how to play a more penetrating game by utilizing the proper strategy and principles that should guide the player in most situations. It begins by outlining and discussing the rules of the game and then proceeds step by step to advance the reader to a new level of playing proficiency.

The book is written in clear, nontechnical language. No matter how good a cribbage player you are, this book will improve your game. It will pay for itself and for the time you spend reading it many times over.

CHAPTER 1   The History of Cribbage

The game of cribbage was invented by the English poet Sir John Suckling (1609–1642). The original spelling of the name was "cribbidge." Initially, the game was played with a deal of five cards, but the modern two-handed game is played with a deal of six cards. Apart from the changes in the spelling of the name, the number of cards dealt, and some terminology, cribbage is today essentially the same game played in Suckling's time.

Charles Cotton, in his classic book *The Compleat Gamester,* written in 1674, referred to the jack in the crib as the "knave noddy." This has led to speculation that the game of cribbage may have had its historical roots in an older game known as *noddy*.

Although little has been recorded about cribbage's origin and early history, the game has been played for over 300 years and has stood the test of time, unlike many other card games in which interest has quickly subsided.

CHAPTER 2   The Rules of Cribbage

If you want to improve your cribbage game your first step is a thorough understanding and mastering of the rules of play. The player must be able to understand the effect of each rule and each possible variation. If you do not know the proper rules for the game, you will be unable to take advantage of the finer points of play. Both beginners and experienced cribbage players should read and study this chapter carefully.

NUMBER OF PLAYERS

Cribbage can be played by two, three, or four players; however, the two-player game is the most common and the most popular.

THE PACK

A regulation pack of fifty-two cards is used. Ranking of cards is from high to low: king, queen, jack, 10, 9, 8, 7, 6, 5, 4, 3, 2, ace. The king, queen, jack, and 10 (commonly referred to as the *10-value* or *tenth cards*) count for a value of ten; the ace has a value of one; and all other cards count their face value.

CRIBBAGE BOARD

Because it is difficult and somewhat confusing to keep score using paper and pencil, the cribbage board is considered standard scoring equipment. It is a rectangular board with four rows of thirty holes, divided by a central panel into two sets of rows. Normally, there are two or four additional holes (called *game holes*) near the starting end of the board to hold the pegs prior to the start of the game.

The rows are divided into six sections of five holes each, an arrangement that aids in pegging and provides bench marks for assessing game progress.

Each player has two pegs of the same color that are used to record scores. Each time the player scores a point, he advances the back peg ahead of the front peg, one hole for each point. The pegging is down the outer row away from the game end of the board and up the inner row. A game of 61 points is once around the outer and inner rows, and a game of 121 points is pegged twice around the outer and inner rows. Some cribbage players refer to rows as *streets;* thus, in a 121-point game, the rows would be *first, second, third,* and *fourth* or *home street.*

THE DRAW

Cards are drawn, and the lowest card deals. If cards of equal rank are drawn, both players draw again.

THE SHUFFLE

The nondealer has the right to shuffle, but the dealer has the right to shuffle last.

THE DEAL

Each player receives six cards, which are dealt one at a time face down, beginning with the nondealer. The turn to deal alternates during the game. Also, the starting deal alternates for each game; that is, the nondealer of the last game would be the dealer for the next game. An exception to this rule, which is observed by some cribbage players, is that the loser deals first; however, this practice is not common.

DISCARDING TO THE CRIB

After looking at the cards in his hand, each player discards two cards into a single pile, thus forming the *crib*. The nondealer must discard first, followed by the dealer. Once the cards have been discarded they can not be picked up by the player. The crib belongs to and counts for the dealer, but it is not exposed or counted until each hand has been played.

THE STARTER

After the players discard cards to the crib, the nondealer cuts the pack, and the dealer turns up the top card of the lower portion of the deck. This card, called the *starter,* is placed face up on top of the complete pack. If the starter is a jack, called *his heels,* the dealer immediately pegs 2 points. In the event the dealer does not peg the 2 points before he plays his first card (after the nondealer plays first), he loses the 2 points. Although the starter is not used in the play of the hand, it is used once by the nondealer in the final count of his hand, twice by the dealer in the final count of his hand, and in the count of the crib.

SCORING

The game must be scored in the following order:

1. "His heels"
2. Pegging in play
3. Nondealer's hand
4. Dealer's hand
5. Dealer's crib

THE PLAY

After the starter is turned up, the nondealer first plays one of his cards face up on the table; the dealer then plays one of his cards, and so on until all cards are played. The players keep their cards in separate piles, and each player must announce the running count total after the play of each card. For example, the nondealer first plays a 4, announcing "Four"; the dealer then plays an 8, announcing "Twelve"; and so on.

THE "GO"

During the play of the cards, the running count total may never exceed thirty-one. If a player is not able to play another card without going over thirty-one, he announces "Go," and the other player may peg 1 point. However, before he can peg the 1 point, he must play any card(s) he can without exceeding thirty-one. If in playing these cards he hits thirty-one, he would peg 2 points instead of the 1 point for the "go."

The player who previously announced the "go" would then lead first, starting a new running count. The remaining cards played by both players would result in a new running count total separate and distinct from the previously played cards.

The dealer is always assured of pegging 1 point for playing the last card unless that card brings the running count to thirty-one, in which case he would peg 2 points.

PEGGING

The term *pegging* refers to the recording of scores on the cribbage board during play. The object during the play of the hand is to peg points by proper play and to prevent your opponent from pegging. During the play of the hand, points may be pegged in any of the following ways:

Jack starter

The dealer pegs 2 points if the starter is a jack.

Fifteen count

Playing a card that makes a count of fifteen scores 2 points.

Pair

Playing a card of the same rank as the card just previously played (4 on 4, Q on Q) scores 2 points.

Threes (also called *triplet* or *pair royal*)

Playing the third successive card of the same rank pegs 6 points.

Fours (also called *double pair royal*)

Playing the fourth successive card of the same rank without exceeding thirty-one pegs 12 points.

Run (also called *sequence*)

Playing a card that when combined with cards previously played forms a run of three or more cards pegs 1 point for each card in the run. The cards making up the run *do not* have to be of the same suit, but they must go strictly by rank. For example, 8–9–10 is a run, but 8–9–J is not.

"Go"

Playing the last card without going over a count of thirty-one scores 1 point.

Thirty-one

Playing a card that makes a count of thirty-one pegs 2 points.
Note: If a player receives a "go" and plays a card for thirty-one, he does *not* receive 1 point for the "go" plus 2 points for making thirty-one. He receives only the 2 points for the thirty-one.

COUNTING THE HAND AND THE CRIB

Following the play of all the cards in the hand, the hands must be counted in the following order:

1. Nondealer's hand
2. Dealer's hand
3. Dealer's crib

During the count of the hand and the crib, the cards must remain spread out on the playing surface so that each card is clearly visible until the other player completely understands the announced count score.

Because the starter is part of each player's hand, the counting hand consists of five cards. Points may be scored in the count of the players' hands and the dealer's crib in any of the following ways:

Fifteen count

Each combination of cards that adds up to fifteen scores 2 points.

Pair

Each pair of cards of the same rank (10–10, *but not* 10–J) scores 2 points.

Threes

Three cards of the same rank (4–4–4, *but not* 10–10–J) scores 6 points.

Fours

The player scores 12 points for four cards of the same rank.

Run

Each card in a run of three or more cards scores 1 point.

Flush

If all the cards in the hand are of the same suit, the player scores 4 points. If all the cards in the hand or the crib are of the same suit as the starter, the player scores 5 points.

GAME

Before the start of the game, the players must agree on whether a score of 61 or 121 constitutes the game. Most players of two-handed cribbage prefer the 121 game because chance and luck in the fall of cards are not as significant in it as they are in the 61 game. The game ends immediately whenever a player reaches the 61 or 121 total whether it is by "his heels," pegging, or counting the hand or the crib (see Scoring). This means that if the nondealer is able to reach 61 or 121 points by the count of his hand, the game is immediately over and the dealer does not have the opportunity to count either his hand or the crib.

LURCH OR SKUNK

In a 61-point game, a *lurch* results when a player has scored 61 points before the other player has scored 31 points; in a 121-point game, when one player has scored 121 points before the other player has scored 91 points. A lurch counts as a double game for the winner provided the lurch agreement has been made between the players before the beginning of the game. A *double lurch* occurs in the 121-point game when a player has scored 121 points before the other player has scored 61 points. A double lurch counts as four games for the winner provided the double lurch agreement has been made by the players before the start of the game.

"MUGGINS"

This is an optional feature of the game. If a player fails to score any points he is entitled to in the play or count of the hand (including the crib), his opponent can declare "Muggins" and claim the overlooked points for his own score. However, the player planning to declare "Muggins" must wait until his opponent has incorrectly pegged his score or until after the opponent's hand has been counted before making the "muggins" declaration and claiming the points. It is recommended that the players agree before the start of the game on whether the "muggins" rule will be in effect.

IRREGULARITIES

There are a number of possible irregularities prior to and during the deal, during the play of the hand, and in the final count of the hand and the crib. The reader should be aware of these irregularities and penalty points.

A dealer's card is exposed in dealing.

Penalty: None; however, the nondealer may call for a new deal
        if he has not looked at any of his dealt cards.

A nondealer's card is exposed in dealing.

Penalty: The nondealer scores 2 points and may call for a new deal *if* he has not looked at any of his remaining dealt cards.

Either player receives less than the correct number of cards.

Penalty: None; however, there must be a new deal.

The nondealer receives more than the correct number of cards.

Penalty: The nondealer scores 2 points if he notices the error before picking up his cards. A new deal is required.

The dealer receives more than the correct number of cards.

Penalty: None; however, the nondealer may either request a new deal or that the dealer spread out his hand face down on the table so that he can select the extra card(s) for removal.

The cards are not dealt one at a time.

Penalty: None; however, there must be a new deal.

A card is "boxed" (face up) in the pack.

Penalty: The "boxed" card is considered an exposed card and handled according to the appropriate procedure for a card exposed in dealing.

Either player announces "go" although able to play additional cards, or either player gets a "go" and fails to play cards in hand that would keep the count under thirty-one.

Penalty: The player may not correct the error once his opponent plays a card. The cards not played are dead, and the opponent scores 2 points.

A wrong running count is announced by either player.

Penalty: None; however, the error must be corrected on demand of the opponent. If the opponent does not notice the error and continues the play of his cards, the error cannot be corrected.

A player refuses to pay a penalty for violation of the rules of play.

Penalty: His opponent may claim the game.

Kibitzers interfere with the progress of a game or help either player.

Penalty: None; however, a player may not request assistance from bystanders or his opponent in the counting of the hand or the crib.

A player makes an error in pegging.

Either player pegs fewer points than he is entitled to.

Penalty: The player may not rectify the error if he has played his next card or if a cut for the next deal has been made. His opponent can claim the overlooked points if "muggins" is in effect.

Either player pegs more points than he is entitled to.

Penalty: His opponent can demand that he rectify the number of points overscored and can add the same number of overscored points to his own score.

A player fails to peg the points for his hand or the crib before returning cards to the dealer for shuffling.

Penalty: The player loses the points to which he was entitled.

One player's hand consists of the incorrect number of cards (after discarding to the crib), but the other hand and crib have the correct number of cards.

Penalty: The other player can call for a new deal or score 2 points and correct the hand by removing extra cards or adding additional cards from the pack.

Both players' hands have the correct number of cards, but the crib has the wrong number of cards.

Penalty: The nondealer scores 2 points, and the crib is corrected by removing extra cards or adding additional cards from the pack.

More than one hand (including the crib) has the wrong number of cards.

Penalty: If a player has the correct number of cards in his hand, he scores 2 points, and there is a new deal.

Once the player has quit the pegs (i.e., removed his fingers from the front peg) when scoring points, the score cannot be changed.

Penalty: None.

Once a card has been played in accordance with the rules of the game, it cannot be recalled and another card played.

Penalty: None.

A player handles his opponent's pegs with the exception of re-positioning them in the appropriate location when the opponent accidentally dislodges both his pegs.

Penalty: His opponent scores 2 points.

A player removes his opponent's front peg.

Penalty: His opponent may claim the game.

A player accidentally dislocates his own front peg.

Penalty: He must place his peg behind the back peg unless both players agree on where peg should be repositioned.

Both players dislocate their own front pegs by accident.

Penalty: Both players must agree on where pegs should be repositioned; otherwise, the game is voided.

Either player handles his own pegs except when he has the legitimate right to score.

Penalty: His opponent scores 2 points.

A player accidentally dislodges both his pegs.

Penalty: There is no penalty *if* the opponent has the right to reposition the pegs in the appropriate location. The opponent may claim the game if this right is denied him.

A player gets his cards mixed up with those of the crib.

Penalty: His opponent scores 2 points, and there is a new deal.

Either player handles the deck following the completion of the deal except to cut for the starter.

Penalty: The opponent scores 2 points.

CHAPTER 3   Instant Visual Recognition of Card Values

The manner in which cards are held in the hand and discarded to the crib is a very important part of the game of cribbage. Too often, the player does not make an accurate and complete analysis of his cards and does not hold and/or discard the proper cards. Because of the fast pace of the game, the player is forced to look at his hand quickly and to make fast decisions on how to play his cards. If he waits too long in making a decision, his opponent may become impatient.

For this reason, it is very important that the serious cribbage player practice to develop his skill at instant visual recognition of his hand to determine what to hold and what to discard. You should attempt to form a mental picture of your hand and all its possible card combinations the instant you pick it up. People who have high numerical aptitude and arithmetic skill will naturally be able to do this faster than others. However, everyone should be able to improve facility in his card reading. This facility is important not only in reading your hand but also in scoring your hand and crib after play. In addition, it will enable you to check the accuracy of the other player's count of *his* hand and crib quickly, allowing you to declare "Muggins" and claim any overlooked points.

Here are some of the ways that you can develop this recognition skill.

Pick up the six dealt cards one at a time rather than all at once. In this way, you will be able to evaluate, carefully and progressively, the rank value of each card in relation to all the other cards in your hand and thus determine the optimum four cards to hold. For many players, the confusion that results from seeing all six cards at one time makes it difficult to evaluate them objectively and to determine what four cards to hold. Remember to pick up your cards *slowly,* one at a time, and not be concerned if your opponent expresses impatience. This is a critical moment and deserves your careful and deliberate attention.

Learn to identify quickly those two cards that add up to fifteen; for example, 6–9; 7–8; 10–5.

Learn to think of certain cards in combination.

1–4; 2–3 = 5
1–5; 2–4; 3–3 = 6
1–6; 2–5; 3–4 = 7
1–7; 2–6; 3–5; 4–4 = 8
1–8; 2–7; 3–6; 4–5 = 9
1–9; 2–8; 3–7; 4–6; 5–5 = 10

In this way, you will not have to count each card individually to make fifteen; you will be able to add up combinations quickly. For example, if you held 1–6–8–8, you would simply combine the 1 and 6 for a count of seven and say "fifteen, two; fifteen, four; and a pair for 6 points." You will not have to take the time to add the 1–6–8 for one fifteen and the second 1–6–8 for the second fifteen and then add the pair.

Remember that a single run may be worth *3* points (9–10–J); *4* points (9–10–J–Q), or *5* points with an appropriate starter (9–10–J–Q–K), plus any additional points for combinations adding up to fifteen, a flush, or "his nobs."

Remember that a double run of three cards is worth *8* points (9–10–10–J), plus any additional points for fifteen combinations or "his nobs."

Remember that a double run of four cards is worth *10* points (9–10–10–J–Q), plus any additional points for fifteen combinations or "his nobs."

Remember that a triple run of three cards is worth *15* points (9–10–J–J–J), plus any additional points for fifteen combinations or "his nobs."

Remember that a quadruple run of three cards is worth *16* points (9–10–10–J–J), plus any additional points for fifteen combinations or "his nobs."

Deal hands to yourself and practice instant visual recognition of your cards. This will help you to master the skill of quick card reading and also to evaluate your hand quickly for purposes of discarding and scoring.

The value of a hand or a crib with the starter can range from 0 points to 29 points. It is impossible for the hand or the crib to have a value of 19, 25, 26, or 27 points. This is why a player who holds a "bust" hand worth 0 points will say that he has "nineteen." The highest possible hand is 5–5–5–J with a starter of 5 that is the same suit as the J.

There are 936,491,920 combinations of hands (six cards) that could be dealt to you in a game of two-handed cribbage. Not even a small percentage of these combinations could be listed in this book. However, here is a list of some random cribbage hands. Figure out the point value of each hand. The correct answers are given on page 17.

RANDOM CRIBBAGE HANDS

These random cribbage hands represent the four cards retained after discarding to the crib plus the starter.

(a) 3–7–7–7–9   (f) 2–3–4–5–5

(b) 2–2–3–4–4   (g) 6–6–7–7–9

(c) 6–6–6–9–9   (h) 2–4–6–7–9

(d) 5–5–5–5–K   (all spades)

(e) 5–8–9–10–Q   (i) 7–8–9–9–9

    (all hearts)   (j) 7–8–8–9–9

(k) J–Q–Q–K–K
(l) 3–3–3–3–9
(m) 2–9–10–10–10
(n) 3–3–3–4–4
(o) 1–2–2–3–3
(p) 6–7–10–Q–K
    (all diamonds)
(q) 2–3–3–9–K
(r) 2–2–K–K–K

(s) 2–3–8–9–10
(t) 3–5–Q–Q–Q
(u) 5–5–10–J–Q
(v) 5–5–5–5–N*
(w) 2–4–4–6–9
(x) N*–Q–K–K–K
(y) 6–7–7–7–8
(z) 2–3–3–Q–Q
    N = his nobs

VALUES OF RANDOM CRIBBAGE HANDS

(a) *6 points:* three 7s (6 points)

(b) *18 points:* one fifteen combination (2 points), quadruple run of three cards (12 points), and two pairs (4 points)

(c) *20 points:* six fifteen combinations (12 points), one pair (2 points), and three 6s (6 points)

(d) *28 points:* eight fifteen combinations (16 points) and four 5s (12 points)

(e) *12 points:* two fifteen combinations (4 points), run of three cards (3 points), and five-card flush (5 points)

(f) *12 points:* one fifteen combination (2 points), double run of four cards (8 points), and one pair (2 points)

(g) *8 points:* two fifteen combinations (4 points) and two pairs (4 points)

(h) *11 points:* three fifteen combinations (6 points) and five-card flush (5 points)

(i) *17 points:* one fifteen combination (2 points), triple run of three cards (9 points), and three 9s (6 points)

(j) *20 points:* two fifteen combinations (4 points), quadruple run of three cards (12 points), and two pairs (4 points)

(k) *16 points:* quadruple run of three cards (12 points) and two pairs (4 points)

(l) *24 points:* six fifteen combinations (12 points) and four 3s (12 points)

(m) *6 points:* three 10s (6 points)

(n) *8 points:* one pair (2 points) and three 3s (6 points)

(o) *16 points:* quadruple run of three cards (12 points) and two pairs (4 points)

(p) *5 points:* five-card flush (5 points)

(q) *8 points:* three fifteen combinations (6 points) and one pair (2 points)

(r) *8 points:* one pair (2 points) and three Ks (6 points)

(s) *5 points:* one fifteen combination (2 points) and run of three cards (3 points)

(t) *12 points:* three fifteen combinations (6 points) and three Qs (6 points)

(u) *17 points:* six fifteen combinations (12 points), run of three cards (3 points), and one pair (2 points)

(v) *29 points:* eight fifteen combinations (16 points), four 5s (12 points), and "his nobs" (1 point)

(w) *8 points:* three fifteen combinations (6 points) and one pair (2 points)

(x) *16 points:* triple run of three cards (9 points), three Ks (6 points), and "his nobs" (1 point)

(y) *21 points:* three fifteen combinations (6 points), triple run of three cards (9 points), and three 7s (6 points)

(z) *12 points:* four fifteen combinations (8 points) and two pairs (4 points)

CHAPTER 4   Determining What Cards to Hold in Your Hand

As a rule, you should attempt to hold the four cards that have the highest value and that offer the maximum chance for improvement when combined with the starter. During most stages of the game, you will want a high-count hand; but toward the end of the game, if you have only a few points to go, you may want a pegging hand.

It is important to remember that approximately 50 percent of the points you score in the average cribbage game will come from the count of the cards in your hand. In studying the following guidelines, remember that they are only suggestions. The decision on what cards to hold in your hand will also depend, to some extent, on whether the crib is yours or your opponent's.

Keep a run of three (8–9–10), splitting a pair if necessary. If the starter matches one card of the run, at least 5 points will be added to the count.

Keep a double run (10–10–J–Q), discarding the other two cards (regardless of value) to the crib. If the starter matches one unpaired card of the double run, a minimum of 8 points will be added to the count; if the starter matches any pair included in the double run, a minimum of 7 points will be added.

Keep cards that combine for a count of five (2–3, 1–4, 2–2–3–3, and 1–4–4–4) because the frequently turned (one time in three) tenth-card starter will significantly improve your total count.

Keep three of a kind (pairs royal) in most instances. If your hand is 2–6–6–6–10–K, hold the 2–6–6–6 for a count of 6 points.

Keep four of a kind (double pairs royal) at all times. If your hand is 3–4–4–4–4–9, discard the 3–9 and hold 4–4–4–4 for a 12-point count.

If you have a choice of cards to hold in your hand, you should always attempt to hold cards that will facilitate scoring thirty-one. For example, suppose you hold A–3–8–J–Q–K. You have a choice of discarding two of the three low cards. The most appropriate discards would be the 3 and the 8. The ace combined with the three tenth cards may combine for a count of thirty-one regardless of which player leads first.

If you have a choice of cards to hold in your hand, hold four cards of the same suit. This will add 4 points (5 points if the starter is of the same suit) to your hand count. Naturally, the consideration of holding a flush should be secondary to holding those cards that have maximum actual and/or potential point value.

CHAPTER 5   Discarding to the Crib

The average cribbage player too often places undue emphasis on holding cards for the highest possible point total in his hand and completely forgets the importance of the cards he discards to the crib (whether his opponent's or his own). Although only an approximate 18 percent of your total points scored in the average cribbage game will come from the count of the crib, these points are critical and make the difference between winning or losing consistently.

Effective cribbage strategy includes the determination of which cards it is appropriate to discard to the crib. Quite often, the choice is an easy one because of the makeup of your hand. For example, if you hold 4–5–6–6–9–K, the choice is quite easy; naturally, you would discard the 9–K to either your own or your opponent's crib and hold the 12-point hand.

It should be emphasized once again that the choice of the two cards to be discarded to the crib depends upon whether the crib is yours or your opponent's. The strategy to be followed in making this very important decision deserves your careful consideration.

The crib counts for the dealer; therefore, the dealer should discard to the crib cards (*helpers*) that are most likely to create a score when combined with the nondealer's discards and the starter. The nondealer should discard cards (*spoilers*) that are least likely to create scoring combinations in the crib.

DISCARDING TO YOUR OPPONENT'S CRIB

Discarding unfavorable cards to the dealer's crib is termed *balking* the crib. The nondealer discards spoiler cards that are least likely to result in a scoring combination, such as fifteen, run, and pair. At the same time that the nondealer is balking the crib, the dealer attempts to *salt* the crib with cards most likely to result in a scoring combination.

Here are some principles you should follow in discarding to your opponent's crib.

Discard cards that are far apart in value because they cannot be used in a run. For example, a favorable discard would be 4–K because the K is a natural killer and, generally, the 4 is too low to be used in a fifteen combination unless the other player discards an ace. However, this is unlikely because the ace is an excellent card to be used in the play of the hand for pegging purposes and is therefore not often discarded to the crib. Another example of a wise discard would be 8–Q. In order to complete the run, the crib would have to contain 9–10–J, including the starter.

Favorable balking cards are the K in combination with 10, 9, 8, 7, 6, or A and the Q in combination with 9, 8, 7, 6, or A. However, you must use discretion in discarding aces because they are especially valuable for pegging during the play of the hand.

Of course, there will be exceptions to this guideline, depending on the six cards that you are dealt. For example, suppose you were dealt 3–4–5–10–J–Q. The hand includes two three-card runs worth 3 points each and three fifteen combinations worth 2 points each. The correct strategy would be to discard the 3 and the 4 and keep the upper run and the three fifteen combinations (5–10–J–Q) for a total of 9 points.

Never discard a 5 to your opponent's crib except under very unusual circumstances. A 5 is a very dangerous card to discard because it can combine with sixteen other tenth cards to make a fifteen count worth 2 points. However, there are times when it is necessary to discard a 5 to your opponent's crib. For example, if you held 4–5–7–8–8–9, you have no alternative but to keep the 7–8–8–9 (12 points, with excellent chances for improvement) and discard the 4 and the 5.

If you have a choice of suits in discarding, put cards of two DIFFERENT *suits in your opponent's crib, thereby preventing the possibility of a flush.*

Do not discard a pair except under very unusual circumstances. For example, if you hold 5–5–7–8–8–9, you have no alternative but to keep 7–8–8–9 (12 points) and discard the two 5s to the crib.

Never discard a jack to your opponent's crib if you can avoid it. The obvious reason for this is that if the jack is of the same suit as the starter, your opponent will gain 1 point.

DISCARDING TO YOUR OWN CRIB

You should naturally give your own crib the cards that are most likely to produce a scoring combination (helpers) while retaining the best possible hand. Remember that your opponent is attempting to discard the worst possible cards (spoilers) to your crib.

Here are some principles you should follow in discarding to your own crib.

If you have a choice of suits in discarding, put cards of the SAME *suit in your crib, thereby increasing the possibility of a flush.*

If you hold a poor hand that offers no real choice of cards to discard, keep cards in your hand that are best for pegging. A good pegging hand consists of four different cards. If you hold an excess of high cards, keep an ace or a 2 for pegging on a possible thirty-one.

The 5, in general, is the most desirable card to discard to your own crib because tenth cards are frequently discarded to the crib by your opponent.

The cards that are normally desirable to discard to your own crib are two 5s, 5 and 6, 5 and tenth card, 2 and 3, 1 and 4, 6 and 9, 7 and 8, and other similar combinations. If you have no comparable cards to discard, try to discard cards that are fairly close in value (2–4, 5–7) so that they might be helped by your opponent's discards or by the starter card.

If you have a choice of cards to discard, discard a jack to your own crib. You will score 1 point if the jack is the same suit as the starter.

A 7 and an 8 are considered very favorable cards to discard. They form a fifteen combination and are also the basis, along with your opponent's discards and the starter, for a run.

CHAPTER 6   Play of the Hand

Leading and playing the correct cards is a very critical phase of cribbage. This is the area that distinguishes the average player from the expert. Approximately 32 percent of your scores will come from the play of your hand and proper pegging. Therefore, as a serious student of the game, you should read and review this chapter very carefully.

OPENING CARD LEADS

The safest opening lead is a 4 or any other card lower than a 5. Because the highest card your opponent can play is a tenth card, this lead prevents him from either making or exceeding a fifteen combination, thereby depriving you of the chance to make it. Of course, your opponent could pair the lead card, but this is the calculated risk that must be taken. It is difficult to set up a defense against having a lead card paired unless you hold more than one of the lead cards, which means that the probability of its being paired by your opponent is lessened. As the nondealer, your first card lead is the most dangerous because you have no clear idea what cards your opponent might be holding.

The most dangerous opening lead is a 5. Any tenth card can be played on it for a fifteen combination, scoring 2 points for your opponent.

Do not be afraid to lead a tenth card. Often, there is a reluctance to lead a tenth card for fear that the other player will counter with a 5 for a fifteen combination. Sometimes this will happen; however, it is important to remember that the other player may have discarded a 5 to his own crib in hopes that you have discarded a tenth card.

If you hold a 5, do not hesitate to lead a tenth card; then if the other player plays a 5 for fifteen, you can counter with your own 5 and score 2 points for a pair. Of course, if your opponent holds two 5s, he could counter for pairs royal and 6 points, but that is the calculated risk you must take. Furthermore, if you hold one or more 5s, you can lead the tenth card knowing that the chances of your opponent holding a 5 are thereby lessened.

The lead of a tenth card is recommended when you hold two or more tenth cards. If your opponent pairs your tenth-card lead or plays any high card, the play of your second tenth card will often result in forcing your opponent to declare "Go."

PLAYING CARDS TOWARD A COUNT OF FIFTEEN

It is normally better strategy to play to make a fifteen combination than to pair your opponent's card. This will eliminate the possibility of your opponent playing the third card and scoring 6 points on threes. The exception to this might be that it would be safer to pair a normal first card lead of a card under 5 on the basis that your opponent is following standard strategy in leading with a safe card that cannot be played on for a fifteen combination.

When you hold a 2 and a 3, or an ace and a 4, lead either card so that you can make a fifteen combination if your opponent plays a tenth card.

LEADING FROM A PAIR

It is usually advisable to lead from a pair unless you hold a pair of 5s. If your opponent should pair your play, you can counter with threes and score 6 points (to his 2 points). Do not hesitate to score threes because there is only a slight chance that your opponent holds the fourth card and can score four of a kind. For example, if you hold 4–4–9–10, the probability that your opponent holds the fourth 4 after you play the third 4 is 1 in 44, or about 2 percent.

Trapping an opponent into pairing a card so that you can make threes is an especially effective lead when the card is 8 or above. In such a situation, your opponent cannot play the fourth card—if he holds it—because it would bring total count above thirty-one.

Although you should never lead from a pair of 5s, it is important during the play of the hand that you quickly play one of the 5s; otherwise you may be caught with and forced into leading the 5.

LEADING FROM A HAND WITH A COMBINATION OF HIGH AND LOW CARDS

If you hold a hand made up of a combination of high and low cards, it is generally advisable to play the high cards first, thus keeping the low cards available for pegging a "go."

Holding high cards in a hand with choice of play.

If you hold a hand made up of high cards (8–9–10–J) and have a choice of play, it is advisable when you play cards that would put the count over twenty-four *to play a card that will make an even (twenty-six, twenty-eight, thirty) rather than an odd (twenty-five, twenty-seven, twenty-nine) total count.* In this way, if your opponent gets a "go," he will not be able to play successively any small pairs he is holding (such as two 3s on a "go" of twenty-five, two 2s on a "go" of twenty-seven, and two As on a "go" of twenty-nine). He would score just 3 points (2 for a pair and 1 for "go") rather than 4 points (2 for a pair and 2 for thirty-one).

LEADING A CARD THAT, IF PAIRED, WILL ALLOW YOU TO PLAY ANOTHER CARD TO MAKE FIFTEEN

When holding a 3 and a 9, lead the 3. If your opponent pairs the 3, you can play the 9 and make fifteen.

When holding a 4 and a 7, lead the 4. If your opponent pairs the 4, you can play the 7 and make fifteen.

When holding a 3 and a 6, lead the 6. If your opponent pairs the 6, you can play the 3 and make fifteen.

When holding an ace and a 7, lead the 7. If your opponent pairs the 7, you can play the ace and make fifteen.

PAIRING YOUR OPPONENT'S LEAD

Pairing the first card lead by your opponent. Be careful of pairing the first lead card by your opponent unless you hold a third card of the same rank. Your opponent may lead one of a pair in the hope that you will pair, so that he can then counter for threes and 6 points. However, if you also hold a pair of the same rank (7 or under), you can then counter for four of a kind and 12 points.

If you have *just one option* of pairing the first card lead by your opponent or starting a run, your decision will be governed by your board position and whether you are playing offensively or defensively. Generally, if you are playing defensively, pair the card and eliminate the possibility of a long run; if you are playing offensively, play the card that builds toward a longer run.

Pairing a card your opponent has played to make fifteen. Whenever your opponent plays a card to make fifteen, you are generally safe in pairing the card he played. In such a situation, he is intent not on setting a trap but rather on making fifteen for 2 points. The *exception* to this guideline is that you should never pair the last card played if it is a 6 because you will make the count twenty-one, which allows your opponent to play a 10 for thirty-one and a "go."

LEADING FROM TWO CARDS THAT TOTAL FIFTEEN

Middle-range cards (6, 7, 8, 9) are hazardous to lead because they provide an opportunity for your opponent to make fifteen. However, if you have more than two middle cards, the lead is not as hazardous because you have other cards with which to build a run. Naturally, whether you want to build the run will depend on whether you are playing offensively or defensively.

When holding a 9 and a 6, lead the 6; if your opponent plays the 9 for a count of fifteen, you can counter with your 9 for a pair with assurance that your opponent cannot play the third 9, even if he holds it, because it would bring the count over thirty-one.

PLAYING A CARD THAT WILL ALLOW YOUR OPPONENT TO COUNTER AND MAKE A DOUBLE SCORE

Never play a card that will enable your opponent to make a double score. Here are some situations you should avoid.

Fifteen and a pair for 4 points. For example, your opponent leads with 9, and you play a 3 for a count of twelve. This gives your opponent a chance to play a 3 for fifteen and a pair. The same reason makes the following plays undesirable:

NEVER PLAY A	FOR A COUNT OF
2	thirteen
3	twelve
4	eleven
5	ten
6	nine
7	eight

Fifteen and a run. For example, your opponent leads with a 4, and you play a 5. Your opponent can then play a 6 for fifteen and a run of three cards for 5 points. Even if you have cards to continue the run, this play is not good strategy because your opponent has picked up an extra 2 points for the fifteen combination.

Thirty-one "go" and a pair for 4 points. For example, you play a 6 on a count of nineteen for a count of twenty-five. This allows your opponent to counter with a 6 for a pair and a thirty-one "go." For the same reason, the following plays are undesirable:

NEVER PLAY A	FOR A COUNT OF
6	twenty-five
7	twenty-four
8	twenty-three
9	twenty-two

LEADING AND PLAYING CARDS TOWARD A RUN

As a general rule, play ON *(i.e., toward a run) when you have close cards, and play* OFF *(i.e., away from a run) when you do not have close cards.* For example, the nondealer leads a 3, and the dealer holds 10–Q–Q–5. It would be unwise to play the 5 because the nondealer could score with a 4 for a run of three cards and the dealer would not have another card with which to counter and extend the run. In this situation, the dealer should play off with one of his other cards.

If you hold a run of three cards (2–3–4), it is advantageous to lead the lowest (2) or highest (4) rather than the middle card of the sequence (3) because there is greater opportunity to extend the run. It is important that you do not allow your opponent the opportunity of adding a card to a run that you cannot continue.

PLAYING TOWARD A COUNT
OF THIRTY-ONE

Keep in mind the importance and advantage of reaching the count nearest to thirty-one ("go") because it is worth 1 point and of making the count exactly thirty-one because it is worth 2 points. Remember that the dealer, as the last to play, has greater opportunity for making a count of thirty-one.

You receive a "go" and have the option of playing one of several cards for the "go." When you receive a "go," it is important to keep in mind the point total on which you received the "go." You are then able to play your remaining cards with some knowledge of the card(s) your opponent may hold in his hand. For example, you receive a "go" on a count of twenty-three, and you hold a 5 and a 7 in your hand. On the basis of knowing that your opponent does not hold a card smaller than a 9, you would play the 7 for the "go" so you could play your remaining 5 on his probable tenth card lead.

Keep a small pair or small cards in sequence for a "go." If you are the dealer (and therefore the last to play) and have a choice of cards to play, attempt to keep a small pair (say, two As, two 2s, two 3s). If your opponent plays out his cards, you will not only get a "go" but also score 2 points with a pair. Also, you may want to keep two small cards in sequence (such as 1–2 or 2–3) so that if you get a "go," you have the possibility of extending a run from your opponent's last card played.

Keep in mind the large number of tenth cards in the deck. Remember that there are sixteen tenth cards in the deck. You should attempt to play your cards under the general assumption that the tenth cards are proportionally represented in your opponent's hand. Lead your opponent into playing a tenth card as follows:

CARD HELD IN HAND	ATTEMPT TO PLAY CARD TO MAKE THE COUNT
(A)	(B)
2	nineteen
3	eighteen
4	seventeen
5	sixteen
6	fifteen

7	fourteen
8	thirteen
9	twelve
10	eleven

By holding the card in column A and playing another card to make the count in column B, if your opponent plays the frequently held tenth card, you can then play the card in column A for a count of thirty-one. Although your opponent may avoid this trap, he is forced into playing a smaller card which could create a problem for you later in the play of the hand.

IMPORTANCE OF PEGGING IN THE HOME STRETCH

Assuming that you are the dealer in what appears to be the last hand of the game (the *home stretch*), your main objective should be to prevent your opponent from pegging points during the play of his hand. You should keep cards in your hand that will allow you to play "off," or defensively. If your opponent's count in his hand is large enough to give him the game, nothing can be done about it. But in the event his hand count is not sufficient, another deal will be required; and you, as the nondealer, will then have the advantage of the first count. Under these circumstances, you would want to hold cards in your hand that are fairly far apart in value. For example, from a 1–3–4–5–7–10 hand, you should discard the 3 and the 5, thereby making it difficult for your opponent to play cards to form a run.

If, toward the end of the game, you are the nondealer and it is apparent that you have enough points in your hand to win the game on the count of your hand, under no condition should you attempt to score a single point by pegging during play. Do not pair your opponent's lead or get trapped into playing a card which may form a run. However, if you lack the required number of points in your hand to win the game on the count of your hand, then you must play "on," or offensively, and attempt to score by pegging. Unless you do this, you probably will not have any chance of winning the game.

WHAT CARDS MAKE A GOOD PEGGING HAND?

Put yourself in your opponent's place when deciding what cards to hold in your hand. You know that he is not going to lead a tenth card for fear of your countering with a 5 for a fifteen combination. Also, he is probably not going to lead with 6, 7, 8, or 9 because you might be able to counter with a card for a fifteen. He will definitely not play a 5 because of the chance that you will play a tenth card for fifteen. This leaves A, 2, 3, and 4 as logical lead cards.

Therefore, a good pegging hand is made up of four different cards. The best four cards to hold for pegging when you are the dealer are A–2–3–4. Of course, it is unlikely that you would be able to hold these four cards at one time, but you should attempt to hold as many as possible.

For example, suppose you are dealing what appears to be the last hand of the game. Your opponent is 5 points from game, and you are 3 points from game. You have to assume that your opponent's hand is worth 7 points on show and enough to win the game. Your strategy has to be able to gain sufficient points in the play of your hand. You know that you will obtain 1 of the points you need by being the dealer because *the dealer is always assured of the last point in pegging.* Now, how do you peg the two additional points? Keep in your hand any A, 2, 3, or 4 for pegging purposes. If you were dealt A–2–4–6–8–10, discard the 8 and the 10. From the A–2–4–6 hand, you will be able to score 2 points if your opponent's lead is A, 2, 4, 6, or 9.

Here is another example. Suppose you are dealing what appears to be the last hand of the game. Your opponent is 5 points from game. You have to assume that his hand is worth 7 points and more than enough to win the game. You must be able to gain sufficient points in the play of your hand to win the game. You hold 2–4–4–8–10–10 in your hand. Split up the two pairs, and keep 2–4–8–10. From this hand, you will be able to peg if your opponent leads a 2, 4, 5, 7, 8, or 10. If you chose to discard the 2 and the 8 in order to retain the two pairs for 4 points, you would be able to peg only against a lead of 4, 5, or 10.

Say you are the dealer and are 2 points short of game. You know that you will obtain 1 point simply by being the dealer because *the dealer is always assured of the last point in pegging.* Your problem is to attempt to gain the important second point by pegging. If you are dealt A–A–A–10–J–Q, keep the A–10–J–Q because you have the opportunity of pairing your opponent's lead of A, 10, J, or Q; you will also have a good chance of making the "go" or thirty-one.

MISCELLANEOUS

Do not play a card that brings the count to five or twenty-one. If your opponent has a frequently held tenth card in his hand, he will score 2 points.

Beware of unusual leads by your opponent. Suppose you are the dealer and your opponent's lead is a 5. You should ask yourself why he would lead a 5 when he knows that there are sixteen tenth cards. Either he has some unusual motive, or he holds four 5s.

Don't play into a trap. Does the other player generally play a given card, say a 3, in hopes that you will play a tenth card, so that he can then counter with a 2 for fifteen? If so, you must do exactly the opposite of what he wants, keeping in mind that he still holds the 2 in his hand. By having knowledge of this one probable card he holds, you have a tremendous advantage in the play of your hand.

CHAPTER 7   Playing "On" or "Off"

The decision to play "on" or "off" is an important part of cribbage. When playing "on," the player is playing offensively and attempting to peg as many points as possible; when playing "off," the player is playing defensively and not attempting to peg points by bulding a run or going for pairs or threes.

The decision to play offensively or defensively is determined primarily by three factors: (1) your board position with respect to your opponent's board position, (2) nearness to the end of the game, and (3) the cards you hold in your hand.

BOARD POSITION

Your *board position* is your game progress considering the number of hands that have been played. On the basis of knowing your actual board position compared with your expected board position and, likewise, of knowing your opponent's actual board position compared with his expected board position, you will be able to decide whether you should play offensively or defensively.

AVERAGE POINT VALUES

By knowing the average point value of the hand (7 points), the average number of points pegged during the play (dealer, 5 points; nondealer, 4 points), and the average point value of the crib (5 points), you can at any time determine whether you are ahead or behind normal point expectancy. As you can see in the Table of Normal Expectancy on the next page, the average point expectancy for the dealer is 17 in any given hand; whereas the average point expectancy for the nondealer is 11 in any given hand. These averages become especially important when deciding on your strategy for the home stretch.

If after two complete hands you have 28 or more points, you are considered at *normal* expectancy; if you are 7 or more points ahead of your opponent, you exceed normal expectancy and should play "off," or defensively.

The dealer has the advantage in a 61-point game; the dealer has a disadvantage in the 121-point game.

PLAYING "ON," OR OFFENSIVELY

When you are behind in a game, it is generally better to play liberally and seize every possible opportunity to score, even though this means that you risk increasing your opponent's score. Because it is normally considered an advantage to be ahead at the start of the game, both players generally will play "on" aggressively during the first few hands.

As a rule, you should play offensively when you are behind in the game. The intensity of the offensive play is determined by how far behind you are. For example, if you are trailing your opponent by 12 points, you have much more to gain by taking the offense than if you are only 4 points behind. Here are the principles to be followed in offensive ("on") play.

If you have the choice between pairing your opponent's card or playing a card that might lead to or continue a run, choose the run.

Lead one of a pair, especially if the pair is 8 or above. If your opponent pairs your lead, you can play your second card for threes and 6 points. If the card value is 8 or above, your opponent will be unable to play the fourth card of the same rank for fours and 12 points, even if he should hold the card, because he would exceed thirty-one.

Table of Normal Expectancy

PLAYER A	Hand No.	Hand	Pegging	Crib	Running Total	PLAYER B	Hand No.	Hand	Pegging	Crib	Running Total
Dealer	1	7	5	5	17		1	7	4		11
	2	7	4		28	Dealer	2	7	5	5	28
Dealer	3	7	5	5	45		3	7	4		39
	4	7	4		56	Dealer	4	7	5	5	56
Dealer	5	7	5	5	73		5	7	4		67
	6	7	4		84	Dealer	6	7	5	5	84
Dealer	7	7	5	5	101		7	7	4		95
	8	7	4		112	Dealer	8	7	5	5	112

The Table of Normal Expectancy shows you how to use your knowledge of average point values to determine where you *should* be at any stage of a game.

After the completion of an even number of hands (i.e., after the second, fourth, sixth, and eighth hands), both players *should* have the *same* running total point count. Therefore, the player who is leading by 7 points or more at these stages should play "off," or defensively; whereas the other player should play "on," or offensively.

After the completion of an odd number of hands (i.e., after the first, third, fifth, and seventh hands), the first dealer for the game *should* be ahead by 6 points. If the game's first dealer is ahead by 13 points or more at these stages, he should play defensively; whereas the other player should play offensively.

Always play the third card for three of a kind, especially if the card value is 8 or above. If the card value is under 8, there is still very little chance that your opponent has the fourth card. When you are behind, you have to take calculated risks.

Lead with a card from one end of a sequence. For example, if you hold 6–7–8–9, lead the 6 or the 9 in an attempt to entice your opponent into playing a card that will support the building of a sequence.

Lead with one of two cards that total five. If you hold a 2 and a 3, play either card in hopes that your opponent will play a tenth card on which you can play the other card for a fifteen combination.

PLAYING "OFF," OR DEFENSIVELY

When you are leading your opponent by 7 points over normal expectancy, you should play defensively because you will want to protect your lead and not risk giving unnecessary points to your opponent. Here are the principles to be followed in playing "off."

Do not pair your opponent's lead, especially if the card is 8 or above. If the card played is under 8 and you hold a pair of the card played, you should pair the lead card. If your opponent plays threes for 6 points, you can play fours for 12 points.

Lead with small cards on which your opponent is unable to score a fifteen. Good lead cards are A, 2, 3, and 4.

Do not play a 9 if your opponent's lead card is 3. Your opponent probably holds two 3s and is hoping that you will pair his lead. If you play the 9 for a count of twelve, you allow your opponent to play his other 3 for fifteen.

Do not play an ace on your opponent's lead of 7. Your opponent probably holds two 7s, and by playing the ace, you allow him to counter with a 7 for fifteen.

Do not play a card on your opponent's lead card that would al-

low him to make a pair and fifteen at the same time. For this reason, you should avoid the following plays:

Do not play	If your opponent's lead is
7	A
6	3
5	5
4	7
3	9

Do not play a card that might lead to or continue a run. For example, if your opponent leads a 4, do not play 2, 3, 5, or 6; instead, play a card that is far apart in value, such as a 9.

If you have only one choice between pairing the opponent's card or playing a card that might lead to or continue a sequence, choose the pair. However (as mentioned at the beginning of this section), when you have more than one option, you should never pair the opponent's lead unless the lead card is under 8 and you hold a pair of cards of the same rank.

Do not play a card that will result in a count of five or twenty-one. Obviously, such a play should be avoided because it would allow your opponent to counter with a tenth card for 2 points.

CHAPTER 8　Finer Points of Play

This chapter provides valuable information that will add precision to your game. The serious cribbage player should thoroughly master the principles outlined here.

ANTICIPATING THE VALUE OF CARDS IN YOUR OPPONENT'S HAND

After the play of each card, it becomes progressively easier to determine what cards probably remain in your opponent's hand. For example, if your opponent plays a 9 first, an ace second, and an ace third, you can probably safely assume that the last unplayed card is an ace, 4, 5, or 6.

Or suppose your opponent leads with a 10, you play a 5 for a count of fifteen, and your opponent then plays a 9 for a count of twenty-four. At this point, you may surmise that the remaining two cards in his hand are part of a run, for example, 8–9, 8–J, or J–Q, or perhaps part of a fifteen combination with the 9 (pair of 6s) or the 10 (pair of 5s).

By watching the cards played by your opponent, you can play your remaining cards more effectively for maximum pegging points. The greater the number of cards played by your opponent, the easier it is to guess what his remaining card(s) might be.

PLAYING STRATEGY WHEN YOU HAVE A REASONABLE CHANCE TO LURCH OR SKUNK THE OTHER PLAYER

If the opportunity to score a lurch presents itself, you will have two alternatives.

▲   You can play normally and not sacrifice any points toward the long-range objective of winning the game.

▲   You can play boldly in an attempt to gain the lurch and thereby win two games. But at the same time, you will be sacrificing points if the lurch is not successful, and this may be costly to you in the long-run objective of winning the game.

For example, a player counting out first may need 14 points to lurch the opposing player. The strategy in this case might be to try for the maximum number of points in the hand as well as to score the maximum number of points in pegging. Such a player is well ahead of the game and would therefore normally play "off," or defensively. But in this particular instance, he is switching his strategy by playing "on," or offensively, in an attempt to lurch the other player.

REMEMBER THAT THERE ARE SIXTEEN TENTH CARDS

Most beginning cribbage players fail to take into account the fact that there are sixteen tenth cards, compared with four cards of every other rank. A tenth card is therefore the most likely starter. Keep this in mind when discarding to both your own and your opponent's crib. *There is a 1-in-3 chance that the starter will be a tenth card.*

IMPORTANCE OF A THOROUGH AND COMPLETE SHUFFLE

Because a cut of the cards is not required in cribbage, it is extremely important that the cards be completely reshuffled after each hand. If they are not, it is possible that cards from a previous hand may cling together, thus causing a nonrandom distribution of cards such as an excess of sequence cards and/or cards that combine for fifteen. The nondealer has the right to shuffle the cards if he desires; however, the dealer has the right to shuffle last.

RELATIVE POSITIONING OF CARDS HELD IN YOUR OPPONENT'S HAND

The manner in which your opponent arranges the cards in his hand may indicate their ranking or sequence. Most players arrange the cards in their hand in rank order, with the lowest-ranking card on either the left (2–3–3–K) or the right (K–3–3–2).

By observing where your opponent removes his cards from his hand you may have a clue to the relative value of the cards he still holds. Suppose you determine that your opponent always arranges his cards in order from lowest on left to highest on right. Then you know that if he plays his extreme-left card, this is the lowest card in his hand. Suppose it is a 9; you then know that he does not have any remaining card below a 9, and this may provide you with an advantage in the play of your remaining cards.

MAXIMUM NUMBER OF CARDS IN A RUN

The maximum number of possible cards that can be included in a single run is seven and are 1–2–3–4–5–6–7 for a running count total of 28 points. However, there can be a total of nine cards in a *back-to-back run* and are 1–2–3–4–5–6–7–2–1 for a running count total of 31 points. (The last seven cards make up a run.)

However, because each player has only four cards in his hand, the important fact to remember is that a continuous run may consume seven of the eight cards held by the players. The chances of this occurring are remote but possible.

It is also important to remember that the cards do not have to be played in sequential order (3–4–5) to form a run. All that is necessary is that three or more cards played consecutively can be combined to form a run.

EXPOSING A CARD WHEN CUTTING
FOR THE STARTER

Under no conditions should either player have the opportunity to catch a glimpse of the card on the bottom of the packet that has been cut for the starter. The knowledge of just this one card provides an advantage in the play of the hand. This is a common violation in many cribbage circles and should be avoided at all costs.

To avoid exposing the card, the nondealer cutting the deck should be required to place the top cut portion of the deck immediately on the playing surface, rather than holding the cut cards at an elevated distance off the playing surface in possible view of either player. The dealer, after turning the starter, should immediately place the bottom cut portion on the previously cut portion, keeping the cards low and parallel to the playing surface. Further, the dealer, when dealing, should hold the cards close and parallel to the playing surface to prevent exposure of the bottom card.

DEALER'S ADVANTAGE IN THE PLAY OF A HAND

The dealer has the advantage in the play of a hand because he plays after his opponent. The average number of points pegged during the play of a hand is 5 for the dealer and 4 for the nondealer. Because the nondealer plays first, he should play defensively to some degree and strive to counter if the dealer scores. For example, the nondealer plays a 6, and the dealer plays a 9 to make fifteen. The nondealer has anticipated this move and counters with a 9 without allowing the dealer to play a card for triplets, because in playing a third 9 the count would exceed thirty-one.

In addition, the dealer enjoys several specific advantages.

▲   Because the dealer is the last to play, he has a greater opportunity to pair or to play a card for fifteen on his opponent's initial lead.

▲   Because he plays last, the dealer has a greater opportunity of playing cards for a count of thirty-one.

▲   The dealer has the opportunity to gain 2 points if the starter is a jack ("his heels").

REMEMBER THE CARDS YOU DISCARD
TO THE CRIB

It is important that you remember the two cards you discard to the crib, whether it is your opponent's or your own. This will enable you to make better plays with the cards you hold in your hand. For example, from a 4–4–4–5–6–6, you discard 4–4 to the crib. If your opponent leads with a 4, pair it with your 4 because you know that the other two 4s are in the crib.

61-POINT VERSUS 121-POINT GAME

As is true in any two-handed card game that combines skill and luck, the more skillful player will end up the winner in the long run. Consequently, if you consider yourself a more accomplished player than your opponent, insist on the 121-point rather than the 61-point game in order to increase your chances of winning. In the 61-point game, the unskillful player may get lucky and be dealt favorable cards while the skillful player is dealt mediocre or poor cards.

In the event that you consider your opponent a better player than yourself, insist on the 61-point game if you have the option.

SCORING CATEGORIES

Of the points scored in the average cribbage game, 50 percent will come from cards held in the hand; 32 percent, from pegging; and 18 percent, from crib cards. These are approximate percentages and do not include any penalty points for rule violations or points scored through "muggins."

CONDITIONS FOR SOUND PLAY

Playing cribbage is like playing any other game of skill. If you wish to be an effective and consistent winner, you must be disciplined and in full control of your emotions so that they will not influence your playing ability. If your play is guided by your emotions rather than by your judgment in applying the principles of sound play, you will rarely be a consistent winner. Here are some things you should keep in mind to help you maintain self-control and be at 100 percent playing efficiency.

Do not drink alcoholic beverages to excess prior to or during the game. Alcohol dulls the senses and affects your judgment. It lowers your inhibitions and encourages you to take chances rather than to follow the precepts of sound play.

Do not become emotionally upset during play. Nothing is gained, and furthermore, your opponent may intentionally be trying to upset you by his mode of play. He may feel that his chances of winning are increased when you become angry and let your emotions rather than reason govern your play.

Do not play when you are tired. You cannot be at your playing best if you are fatigued and not in top mental and physical condition. In tournament play especially, it is recommended that you attempt to relax prior to a game.

Do not play when you are upset by personal problems. If you have had a bad day (perhaps you are upset by something that happened at work), you should refrain from playing. However, if you are scheduled to participate in league play, you have no alternative but to play. Under these circumstances, you should give yourself a pep talk and attempt to overcome your upset and negative feelings.

Assume a relaxed and carefree playing attitude. A relaxed attitude will have a positive effect on your game; an overly tense and concerned attitude will have a negative effect. Try to relax mentally; if you feel that you are tightening up during play, take a break. Perhaps a cup of tea will help you to relax.

Play with the attitude that you are going to win. By blocking out any negative thoughts, you create within yourself the right winning attitude. Be at your playing best, and follow the best techniques of sound play. If you go into a game lacking confidence in your ability to win, you stand a good chance of losing that game.

Do not complain about your bad luck. Nothing is more self-defeating than complaining about the way the cards are falling. True, there will be times when the other player gets an amazingly good run of cards and starters cut for him. However, keep in mind that the skillful player will come out on top in the long run. By complaining, you will only upset yourself and your playing style.

CHAPTER 9   Cribbage Psychology

Psychology in cribbage can be used to advantage in analyzing the playing habits and mannerisms of an opponent. This is not to say that there are foolproof rules that can be followed with 100 percent accuracy, but if you are alert, you can observe some interesting and revealing things about the other player.

YOUR OPPONENT HESITATES IN DISCARDING CARDS TO THE CRIB

For example, suppose you observe that when your opponent holds a very rich mixture of cards (6–6–7–7–8–8) he always hesitates in choosing what cards to discard to the crib. You can then make the assumption that whenever he hesitates in the same way, he has a barn-burner of a hand.

Conversely, the tricky player may purposely hesitate in discarding cards to the crib from a weak hand (2–4–6–8–10–K) in an attempt to deceive his opponent into believing that he has an extremely good hand and just cannot make up his mind what to discard. This type of play is calculated to put an opponent on the defensive so that he will play his cards according to what he thinks the other player has in his hand.

PLAYING AGAINST AN OPPONENT WHO IS FAMILIAR WITH CRIBBAGE STRATEGY

In any game of skill, there are effective principles of play such as those outlined in this book. If an opponent is familiar with some of these playing strategies, it makes for a tougher game. However, if you know that your opponent always leads a 4 when he holds an A, hoping that you will play a tenth card so that he can counter with the A for fifteen, you have an advantage. How? Instead of playing a tenth card, you will be able to choose to play some other card, all the while remembering that he still holds an A in his hand. The knowledge of this one card that he may be holding provides you with an advantage in the play of the rest of your cards.

HABITUAL PLAY BY AN OPPONENT

Try to determine if your opponent always plays methodically without varying his playing strategy. If so, his style of playing becomes predictable and easier to figure out.

Does your opponent pair your lead card only when he holds two cards of the same rank? This player is probably hoping that you will play threes so that he can play four of a kind for 12 points.

Does your opponent intentionally allow himself to be trapped into a run? He may give the impression in voice and in manner that he is being suckered into the play, but he knows exactly what he is doing. He wants to see the run added to so that on his next play he can play another card to extend the run.

Does your opponent always lead from a pair in anticipation that you will pair the card so that he can counter and play threes? If so, be cautious in pairing his lead card, especially if it is an eight or higher.

KEEP YOUR OPPONENT GUESSING

An important principle to remember in playing your hand is to play the card that keeps your opponent guessing about the other cards you hold in your hand. Furthermore, if you lead or play cards that keep your opponent on the defensive, you will force him to play cards that he would like to use to trap you. Do not fall into habitual patterns of play; try to prevent your opponent from predicting your style and manner of play.

MANNERISMS AND PECULIAR HABITS OF AN OPPONENT

Be alert to the telltale observable behavior of your opponent. Make a mental note of your opponent's mannerisms and style of play. After a game, some cribbage veterans actually make a written record of these observations. Such information is invaluable in future games. The more information you have on an opponent's playing strengths and weaknesses, the greater your advantage.

YOUR OPPONENT QUICKLY DISCARDS TO THE CRIB

If your opponent quickly discards to the crib, he may hold a fairly good hand. For example, from a 2–4–5–5–6–8 hand, the obvious discards would be 2 and 8, and he would retain the 4–5–5–6 hand worth 12 points. Or if dealt 3–6–10–10–J–Q, he would hold the 10–10–J–Q worth 8 points, and discard the 3 and 6. Likewise from a 2–4–7–8–8–8 dealt hand, the decision on the 2 discards is quite evident; he would quickly discard the 2 and 4 and hold the 7–8–8–8 hand, valued at 12 points.

CONVERSATION DURING PLAY

Some opponents will use conversation during play as a propaganda technique to try to influence and/or modify your play. Here are some commonly used conversation techniques.

▲ Your opponent may complain about the cards he has been dealt, when actually he holds very good cards.
▲ He may complain about having such a tough decision to make in discarding to the crib.
▲ He may express surprise or delight with the starter card cut.

If your opponent engages in such behavior, he is simply trying to confuse and frustrate you. Learn to interpret the real meaning behind his words and tone, or better yet, disregard what he says.

To prevent your opponent from gaining any edge, avoid giving him any verbal clues. The best way you can do this is by keeping conversation to a minimum during play.

CHAPTER 10   Beware of Cheating

Because cribbage is a head-to-head game and because there is no cut of the cards by the nondealer, it creates some unique opportunities for cheating. In the great majority of the games you will play, there will be no cheating; nevertheless, the serious cribbage player should be aware of the possible cheating techniques. This knowledge can make the difference between winning and losing. Without it, the most expert cribbage player does not stand a ghost of a chance against even the mediocre cribbage cheater.

The important point to remember is that if you detect cheating, you should complete the game but refuse to play against this person in any future games. In tournament play, refusal may be difficult; and you may want to call your suspicions to the attention of the tournament officials, who will then be able to audit carefully the play of the alleged cheater.

There are many different ways of cheating at cribbage. This chapter outlines only the most popular techniques that the author has observed over many years of play. The interested reader can research the subject in far greater detail by consulting many other excellent reference books available.

The purpose of this chapter is to make the reader generally aware of the dangers of playing against a cheating opponent and to provide some very general guidelines on how to detect cheating.

MARKED CARDS

Marked cards are easily purchased at any magic or novelty store or by mail from supply firms specializing in crooked gambling goods.

Beware of the person who always brings his own deck of cards to the game, using the excuse that he "can't play without a fresh deck."

It is easy to see the advantage marked cards would give a player when you are first to discard to the crib. After seeing the two cards you discarded, he could discard the two cards that would produce a high-scoring crib. For example, if he determines from looking at the backs of your discards to his crib that you have discarded the Q and the 4, he would perhaps discard a 2 and a 3, which would produce a high-scoring crib.

His knowledge of the cards you hold would give him a tremendous advantage in the play of the hand. Be suspicious of an opponent who appears to be overly interested in looking at the backs of the cards you hold in your hand or discard to the crib.

If you suspect that you are playing with marked cards, there are several things you should do.

▲ Hold your cards in your palm so that the opposing player cannot see the backs.

▲ When you are the nondealer and are required to discard first, place the 2 cards, one on top of the other, and discard to the crib so that the back of just 1 card is visible. When you are the dealer, do not discard to the crib until after your opponent has done so.

▲ Do not play any further cribbage with this player. Even if you play with a new deck, he will probably use other cheating techniques.

STACKING THE DECK

When picking up the cards for his next deal, the cheater can easily arrange desirable cards from previously played hands and the crib so that he will deal them to himself on the next round. By interlacing the desirable cards with other cards in the deck and riffling the deck in such a way that these twelve cards remain on the top, he can deal a very good hand to himself and a very poor hand to his opponent. Also, by knowing the value of the six cards his opponent holds, he can make a pretty good guess what cards the opponent will discard to the crib.

The fact that there is no cut in cribbage makes this cheating technique very easy. The cheater simply picks up the cards in the order desired, incompletely riffles the deck, and deals the cards to his unsuspecting opponent. Generally, he will use this technique only once or twice during a game in order to avoid suspicion.

You can protect yourself against this cheating technique by requesting to shuffle the deck before the dealer does. You have this right under the rules of play.

BRIDGE CRIMP TECHNIQUE

When the cheater is the dealer, he can easily get his unsuspecting opponent to turn up the starter he desires. Assuming that the cheater uses the deck-stacking technique, he deals himself a choice hand and holds 4–5–5–6. He would like to have a 4, 5, or 6 as the starter. How does he go about arranging this? Before the deal, he would plant the desired card, say, six or seven cards from the bottom of the deck. Then when he would bridge crimp all cards above that card by slightly bending them lengthwise down the center, with the result that when the clump of cards is placed face down on top of the desired starter card, the center of the clump will not touch the desired starter. The other player will generally cut the deck so that the desired starter card becomes the top card on the lower portion of the deck.

SHORT DECK

This is a very simple cheating technique. All the cheater has to do is leave one or two cards in the box when he breaks open a new deck at the start of the game. He can also simply remove one or two cards from the deck during the game.

By knowing which cards are thus "dead," the cheater has a big advantage in the play of his hand.

You can protect yourself against this cheating technique by counting the deck before the start of play and periodically during the game.

COLLABORATION WITH A KIBITZER

The cheater who uses this technique has an onlooker signaling to him what cards the other player holds. There are a multitude of ways that this can be done. To protect yourself against this cheating technique, be suspicious of any kibitzer, particularly if he spends all his time in back of you outside your range of vision.

PEEKING AND THE USE OF SHINERS

By placing a shiner on the table, the cheater can see the values of cards as they are dealt. Commonly used shiners are polished cigarette lighters, rings, eyeglasses, and the like.

CHEATING ON THE COUNT

The cheater simply overcounts the value of his hand and crib or pegs more points than he is entitled to during the play of the hand. The "muggins" option discourages the use of this cheating technique to some extent but does not eliminate it completely. To prevent cheating on the count, insist that your opponent leave all his cards face up until you have had an opportunity to count them yourself. Also, check the number of holes your opponent pegs after the count to make sure that he does not peg more points than he has actually scored.

CHAPTER 11   The Future of Cribbage

More and more people are playing cribbage and expressing tremendous interest in participating in competitive play as members of cribbage clubs or teams in organized cribbage leagues.

Organized cribbage clubs and leagues exist throughout the United States and Canada and are growing in numbers as the interest in cribbage continues to accelerate. Cribbage clubs or teams engaging in league play are often sponsored by business firms, fraternal organizations, and similar groups. League play generally runs from October to May. Participating teams may be divided into divisions, and a world series-type play-off takes place at the end of the year to determine the league team champion. There may also be a play-off between the top player on each team to determine an individual league champion.

During the course of writing this book, the author contacted a number of cribbage players and great interest was expressed in a national cribbage organization. Final plans have been made to meet this need, and steps have been taken to establish the North American Cribbage Association (NACA).

The association will function as the official representative body for member cribbage players in the United States, Canada, and other countries. It will serve as the official spokesman with respect to rules and regulations governing the game of cribbage, thus ensuring uniform standardized play. The association will promote and stimulate interest in cribbage by coordinating sectional, regional, and national tournaments. A membership directory of individual players and cribbage clubs and leagues will be compiled for members.

The NACA will maintain a rating system for the ranking of players similar to the system used in bridge and chess. Master points will be awarded to participants of league and tournament play.

In addition, the NACA will prepare and distribute to members a periodic cribbage newsletter offering comprehensive coverage of news of interest to cribbage players, including a calendar of forthcoming cribbage tournaments; activities of sectional cribbage clubs and leagues; information on how to organize teams and cribbage clubs; interpretations of the standard rules of play; and other timely subjects, such as strategy for three-handed and four-handed cribbage and the use of extrasensory perception in cribbage play.

For further information on membership and activities of the North American Cribbage Association, write to:

North American Cribbage Association
P. O. Box 20440
Minneapolis, Minnesota 55420